GCSE Music Listening Tests

Teacher's Guide

Ian Burton

www.rhinegoldeducation.co.uk

Music Study Guides

GCSE, AS and A2 Music Study Guides (AQA, Edexcel and OCR)
GCSE, AS and A2 Music Listening Tests (AQA, Edexcel and OCR)
GCSE, AS and A2 Music Revision Guides (AQA, Edexcel and OCR)
AS/A2 Music Technology Study Guide (Edexcel)
AS/A2 Music Technology Listening Tests (Edexcel)
AS/A2 Music Technology Revision Guides (Edexcel)

Also available from Rhinegold Education

GCSE and AS Music Composition Workbooks
GCSE and AS Music Literacy Workbooks
Baroque Music in Focus, Film Music in Focus, Musicals in Focus
Music Technology from Scratch
Understanding Popular Music
Careers in Music

First published 2010 in Great Britain by
Rhinegold Education
14–15 Berners Street
London W1T 3LJ, UK
www.rhinegoldeducation.co.uk

© Rhinegold Publishing Limited 2010
a division of Music Sales Limited

All rights reserved. No part of this publication may be reproduced, stored in a retrieval system, or transmitted in any form or by any means, electronic, mechanical, photocopying, recording or otherwise, without the prior permission of Rhinegold Education.
This title is excluded from any licence issued by the Copyright Licensing Agency, or other Reproducion Rights Organisation

Rhinegold Education has used its best efforts in preparing this guide. It does not assume, and hereby disclaims, any liability to any party for loss or damage caused by errors or omissions in the guide whether such errors or omissions result from negligence, accident or other cause.

You should always check the current requirements of the examination, since these may change. Copies of the OCR specification can be downloaded from the OCR website at www.ocr.org.uk or may be purchased from OCR Publications, PO Box 5050, Annesley, Nottingham, NG15 0DL.
Telephone: 0870 870 6622   Email: Publications@ocr.org.uk

OCR GCSE Music Listening Tests: Teacher's Guide
Order No. RHG264
ISBN: 978-1-907447-01-3

Exclusive Distributors:
Music Sales Ltd
Distribution Centre, Newmarket Road, Bury St Edmunds,
Suffolk IP33 3YB, UK
Printed in the EU

CONTENTS

INTRODUCTION 4

TRACK ORDER 5

ANSWERS 7

    AREA OF STUDY 2: SHARED MUSIC 7

    AREA OF STUDY 3: DANCE MUSIC 17

    AREA OF STUDY 4: DESCRIPTIVE MUSIC 27

    CROSS AREA OF STUDY QUESTIONS 37

FULL TRACK LISTING 40

INTRODUCTION

This teacher's guide is designed to support *GCSE Music Listening Tests* for the OCR specification. Here you will find suggested answers to all of the questions, along with information about the tracks used. A full track listing is given at the back of this guide (page 40).

Please note that there is no CD to accompany this book. All of the tracks used for these tests are available to download from iTunes as one playlist. To purchase and download the playlist, please go to the book webpage on the Rhinegold Education website, where you will find a direct link to the playlist (go to www.rhinegoldeducation.co.uk and search for the OCR GCSE Music Listening Tests).

OCR GCSE Music Listening Tests uses 44 different tracks. You must acquire all of the tracks to complete all of the questions, but you may of course be selective about which questions (and therefore which tracks) you use. Although the iTunes recordings are recommended as the questions have been written with them specifically in mind, you can instead use recordings from other sources, such as CDs or online music players.

It is up to you to decide how to distribute the tracks once they have been downloaded from iTunes. If you need to carry the tracks around with you, you could burn them to a CD or DVD, download them to your iPod, iPhone, or other MP3 player or transfer them to a USB memory stick.

TRACK ORDER

A full track listing, with information about the composer, artist and album for each track, can be found on page 40. The titles given below exactly match the 'Name' of each piece in iTunes (correct at the time of going to print). This track order will allow you to find quickly the relevant track for each test in your iTunes iMix, and to see the timings of each excerpt.

AREA OF STUDY 2: SHARED MUSIC

1.	Test 1.	Piano Concerto No. 4 in G, Op. 58: II. Andante con moto	0:00–0:44, 1:25–2:53
2.	Test 2.	Concerto Grosso in D major Op. 6, No. 5: Menuet: Un poco larghetto	0:00–1:15
3.	Test 3.	Freddie Freeloader	0:21–1:30
4.	Test 4.	A. Dichterliebe, Op. 48: 9. Das ist ein Flöten und Geigen	0:00–1:07
5.		B. Dichterliebe, Op. 48: 7. Ich grolle nicht	0:43–1:40
6.		C. Dichterliebe, Op. 48: 15. Aus alten Märchen winkt es	0:00–0:55
7.	Test 5.	Bubaran: Nudan Mas	0:00–2:08
8.	Test 6.	III. Allegretto	7:36–8:47
9.	Test 7.	Hallelujah	0:00–1:02, 1:58–3:37
10.	Test 8.	Raga Mishra Gara: Gat in Fast Teen Taal	0:00–1:25
11.	Test 9.	Messiah, HWV 56: 15. Chorus: Glory to God in the Highest	0:00–1:06
12.	Test 10.	Captain Courageous	0:00–1:25, 4:40–6:20
13.	Test 11.	One Day Like This	0:00–1:20, 3:15–4:44
14.	Test 12.	A. Bubaran: Nudan Mas	1:03–2:08
15.		B. Messiah, HWV 56: 15. Chorus: Glory to God in the Highest	0:54–1:53
16.	Test 13.	A. Dichterliebe, Op. 48: 7. Ich grolle nicht	0:00–0:59
17.		B. Concerto Grosso in D major Op. 6, No. 5: Menuet: Un poco larghetto	1:15–2:54
18.		C. III. Allegretto	0:00–1:20

AREA OF STUDY 3: DANCE MUSIC

19.	Test 14.	Phuchal	0:00–1:24
20.	Test 15.	Asturian Way	0:00–0:31
21.	Test 16.	A. For an Angel (Radio Mix)	0:00–1:04
22.		B. Rebelión	0:33–1:36
23.		C. Angel	0:19–1:42
24.	Test 17.	Santa Maria (del Buen Ayre)	0:00–1:36
25.	Test 18.	A. Achy Breaky Heart	0:00–1:11
26.		B. Swan Lake, Op. 20, Scene 2: Danses des cygnes – Valse	0:00–0:52
27.	Test 19.	Night Fever	0:00–1:25

28.	Test 20.	**A.** Mi Na Nollag (Double Jigs, Slip Jig)	0:00–0:29
29.		**B.** Asturian Way	1:32–2:02
30.	Test 21.	Gold and Silver (Waltz), Op. 79	1:17–2:30
31.	Test 22.	**A.** He's a Pirate	0:00–1:30
32.		**B.** He's a Pirate (Tiësto Remix)	3:15–4:43
33.	Test 23.	Micaela	3:02–4:45
34.	Test 24.	Libertango	0:56–2:05

AREA OF STUDY 4: DESCRIPTIVE MUSIC

35.	Test 25.	Berlin Foot Chase	0:45–1:42, 2:41–3:58
36.	Test 26.	A Call to Adventure (Theme from Mummy 3)	0:20–1:14
37.	Test 27.	Symphony No. 7, "Sinfonia antartica": I. Prelude: Andante Maestoso-Lento-Poco Animato-Piu Mosso-Tranquillo-Andante… – Largamente	1:26–3:20
38.	Test 28.	Danse Macabre, Op. 40	0:43–2:25
39.	Test 29.	**A.** Main Title	0:00–1:08
40.		**B.** Hellboy & Liz	1:51–2:46
41.		**C.** Stand By Your Man	1:07–2:34
42.	Test 30.	Where Eagles Dare (Film Theme)	0:00–1:27, 1:28–3:09
43.	Test 31.	**A.** The Planet Krypton	0:18–1:22
44.		**B.** Lex Luthor's Lair	0:00–1:30
45.		**C.** Prelude and Main Title March	3:59–4:54
46.	Test 32.	Peer Gynt Suite No. 1, Op. 46: IV. In the Hall of the Mountain King	0:00–2:09
47.	Test 33.	Capsule in Space	0:00–2:46
48.	Test 34.	Pictures at an Exhibition: II. Gnomus	0:49–2:21

CROSS AREA OF STUDY

49.	Test 35.	**A.** Micaela	0:00–0:45
50.		**B.** Symphonie fantastique, Op. 14: IV. Marche au supplice	5:42–7:02
51.		**C.** Raga Mishra Gara: Gat in Fast Teen Taal	3:49–5:03
52.	Test 36.	**A.** Nikosi Sikelela	1:47–3:04
53.		**B.** Danse Macabre, Op. 40	5:05–6:14
54.		**C.** He's a Pirate (Tiësto Remix)	4:01–5:23

ANSWERS

The answers given here are intended as a guide – they are not always the only possible responses. Alternative answers should always receive credit if they form an accurate and unambiguous response to the question.

AREA OF STUDY 2: SHARED MUSIC

TEST 1

Beethoven: Piano Concerto in G, Op. 58 No. 4. (Andante con moto) 0:00–0:44, 1:25–2:53

a. i. Monophonic   **ii.** Homophonic

b. Any two comparisons from:

- Strings = *f*/loud, piano = *p*/soft
- Strings = staccato/jerky, piano = legato/smooth
- Strings in minor key. Piano starts minor, moves to major then returns to minor
- Strings in strict tempo (apart from slight hold back at end). Piano tempo generally feels slower, with use of rubato.

c. Turn

d. Possible answers include:

- Strings start loud but gradually get quieter, as though tamed by the piano
- Piano stays gentle, and gradually tames the more aggressive strings – piano gets slightly more dominant and confident towards the end
- The instruments start to overlap, unlike in extract A, where they are totally separate
- In general, the gaps between the two groups playing are much shorter than in extract A (although there are some more extended piano sections)
- There is a more obvious element of call and response/question and answer.

TEST 2

Handel: Concerto Grosso in D, Op. 6 No. 5 (Menuet) 0:00–1:15

a.

b. Dominant

c. Binary

d. *Either* dynamics are quieter *or* harpsichord part is more elaborate

e. Bar 7, G♯; bar 19, second E

f. Harpsichord; playing chords to fill out the harmony; improvising to decorate the music. Cello/bass/bassoon playing the bass line.

g. Same melody as bars 1–8; new running bass line added; repeat features wind instruments

h. Handel, Bach or another composer from this period

TEST 3

Miles Davis: 'Freddie Freeloader' from *Kind of Blue*   0:21–1:30

a. $\frac{4}{4}$

b. i.

I^7	I^7	I^7	I^7	IV^7	IV^7	I^7	I^7	V^7	IV^7	I^7	I^7

This chord sequence is heard twice more during the extract, although with slight chord changes (mainly at the end of the sequence).

    ii. 12-bar blues

c. i. Piano

ii.	Instrument accompanying the solo	Description of the music played by this instrument
1.	Bass	■ Walking bass ■ Pizzicato/plucked.
2.	Drum kit	■ Swing/swing rhythms (especially on the hi-hat cymbal) ■ Occasional use of snare drum to accentuate particular sections.

d. Possible answers include:

- Other instruments take solos in turn (e.g. trumpet and sax)
- Improvised solos
- All play the main tune/head to finish the piece.

Transcriptions of the solos on this recording are readily available for free on the internet – do a Google search for 'Freddie Freeloader transcription'.

TEST 4

Extract A – Schumann: 'Das ist ein Flöten und Geigen' from *Dichterliebe* 0:00–1:07
Extract B – Schumann: 'Ich grolle nicht' from *Dichterliebe* 0:43–1:40
Extract C – Schumann: 'Aus alten Märchen winkt es' from *Dichterliebe* 0:00–0:55

a.

Features of the time/rhythm	
The music is in $\frac{6}{8}$ time	C
The music is in $\frac{4}{4}$ time	B
The music is in $\frac{3}{8}$ time	A
The performers make extensive use of rubato	B
Features of the relationship between voice and piano	
The piano plays its own melody, quite different to the voice part	A
The piano and the voice share the main melody	C
The melody is in the voice part, and the piano plays repeated chords to support it	B
Other features	
The extract is in strophic (verse) form	A
The music starts in a minor key and modulates to a major key – it does this several times	A
The vocal melody rises gradually over almost two octaves to build to a climax	B

b. Baritone

c. Schumann, Schubert or similar

TEST 5

'Bubaran: Nudan Mas' from *Java Court Gamelan* 0:00–2:08

a. Indonesia/Southeast Asia/Java (which it actually is)/Bali

b. Credit for suitable description of: metallophones; gongs; drums

> The two-headed wooden drums are called kendhang.

c. Possible answers include:

- Solo introduction before everyone comes in with the gong
- Short, core melody in the middle range, repeated over and over again
- Other instruments play different versions of the same melodic pattern
- Higher-pitched instruments (metallophones) play faster patterns
- The large gong marks the end of each cycle
- The music is based around repeated cycles
- Heterophony
- The drum player controls the tempo
- The instruments are tuned to a non-western scale (here the *pélog* scale is used, although it is hard to be certain just by ear as, characteristically, not all of the seven notes are used).

TEST 6

Mozart: Piano Quartet in E♭ (Allegretto) 7:36–8:47

a. Music for a small group of performers; usually one per part; suitable for performance in a small venue

b. Piano; violin; viola; cello

c. Quartet

d. Possible answers include:

- Piano plays on its own
- Srings play on their own
- Piano plays the melody, strings accompany (with held chords or repeated quavers)
- Upper strings play the tune (in 3rds at times) over a cello bass line
- The four instruments come in one after the other – they imitate each other
- The three strings as a group imitate the piano
- Piano plays fast scale passages or arpeggios while the strings play chords (sustained or short)
- All instruments play strong chords together (e.g. at the end).

e. Perfect

f. Mozart, Haydn or similar

TEST 7

Alexandra Burke: *Hallelujah* 0:00–1:02, 1:58–3:37

a.

b. bar 14: IV, V; bar 16: IV

c. Because the chords match the words sung at that point

d. Arpeggios

e. Perfect

f. It modulates to a key one tone higher than extract A

g. Possible answers include:

- Cymbal-roll crescendo at the start
- Much fuller accompaniment, e.g.:
  - Drum kit plays steady quavers, cymbals accentuate
  - String countermelody.
- Last verse is sung/played at a higher dynamic level

- Vocal melody changes and goes higher
- Improvised, ecstatic, gospel-feel to the soloist…
- …Especially when singing over the backing singers
- Backing singers, in harmony, take over the main tune at the climax
- Addition of bells
- Hallelujah section repeated to emphasise climax
- Long-held string notes/glockenspiel over quiet ending.

TEST 8

Ravi Shankar: 'Raga Mishra Gara: Gat in Fast Teen Taal' from *Spirit of India*   0:00–1:25

a. Possible answers include:

Instrument	Role in the music?	How does the musician know what to play?
Sitar	Plays melodic lines	■ Agrees with the other musicians to base the performance on a particular raga (a type of scale, often different going up and coming down, associated with a particular time of day, season or mood) ■ Improvises and develops musical phrases within this raga ■ Sometimes plays a fixed composition associated with the same raga ■ Sometimes enters into dialogue and imitates the rhythm patterns played by the tabla.
Tabla	Plays rhythmic patterns	■ Agrees with the other musicians to base the performance on a particular tala (a cycle of beats) ■ Improvises rhythm patterns within this tala ■ Sometimes enters into dialogue and imitates the melodic shapes and rhythm patterns played by the sitar.
Tanpura	Plays a constant drone all the way through and provides a harmonic base for the performance	■ Plays one or two notes (or a short pattern) as a drone all the way through, based on the most important notes of the agreed raga.

b. Ravi Shankar, Alla Rakha, or another famous sitar/tabla player

This extract is based around raga mishra gara and teental (a 16-beat tala cycle).

TEST 9

Handel: 'Glory to God in the highest' from *Messiah*   0:00–1:06

a. Soprano; alto; tenor; bass

b. Possible answers include:

Words	Musical texture
Glory to God in the highest	■ Homophonic/chordal texture ■ Voices sing together at the same time in harmony ■ String instruments play semiquavers/scale patterns ■ High voices only (soprano, alto, tenor).
And peace on earth	■ Monophonic texture ■ Male voices (tenor/bass only) singing together at the same time ■ In octaves/unison ■ String (quaver/chugging) chords at the end.
Goodwill towards men	■ Contrapuntal/polyphonic texture ■ Fugue (credit reference to imitation, round, etc.) ■ Voices come in one after the other (bass, tenor, alto, soprano) ■ Voices come together at the end.

c. Any two from:

- High sounds (voices and instruments) with no bass for 'glory to God in the highest'
- Low sounds for 'peace on earth'
- Music becomes quiet for the word 'peace' and is loud on the word 'glory'
- The rising interval on the word 'goodwill' sounds uplifting
- The fact that the word 'goodwill' is repeated so many times by different voices and at different pitches (as part of the fugal texture) sounds like goodwill being spread out to all people.

d. Watch and follow a conductor   **e.** Handel, Bach or another composer from this period

TEST 10

Arnie Somogyi's Ambulance: 'Captain Courageous' from *Accident and Insurgency*   0:00–1:25, 4:40–6:20

a. $\frac{4}{4}$

b. Any two from:

- Pizzicato
- Repeated pattern/ostinato/riff, but with slight rhythmic alterations
- Based around only three different pitches.

AREA OF STUDY 2: SHARED MUSIC

c. Possible answers include:

- Sampled sound of crunching/walking across a shingled beach at the start (looped and manipulated so it is in time with the main beat)
- This sampled sound is manipulated through panning so that it walks from left to right speaker
- Other sampled sounds near the start of the extract, such as squeaks, seagulls, chains
- Some students may hear the melodica as an electronic/sampled sound – although it isn't, it could be, and so should access a mark.

d. **i.** Soloist   **ii.** Accompanying another soloist/comping

e. Walking bass

f. Extract B: starts at the same tempo as extract A; then changes to a faster tempo; then returns to the original tempo (of extract A); then changes back to the faster tempo.

The band leader has said that 'the changes in feel and tempo on this tune were completely spontaneous'.

g. Improvisation; off-beat/syncopation; swing rhythms

h. Possible answers include:

i.
- Performers are working together to present the main tune/head – no one player is most important
- Players will have rehearsed this section and agreed in advance how it goes
- Melody instruments (sax and trumpet – often known as 'horns') play the tune
- Rhythm section (bass/piano/drums) provides support.

ii.
- Performers take turns to improvise a solo, and this makes them the most important person in the band at that point
- Rhythm section provides support but, as solos will be different for every performance, they have to listen closely to follow what the soloist does
- All performers, including the rhythm section, have the chance to solo while other members of the band support
- The melody instruments (horns) often do nothing while they wait their turn to solo.

i. Credit for answers which show understanding that:

- This is not notated music – the musicians will probably have learned it by ear/aurally
- The performance will have been developed through improvising, although the main tune at the start has probably been pre-composed, perhaps by one member of the band
- There is often a basic chord structure or ground plan that the performers will learn and then build improvisations over
- Different performers take the lead at different times, and the others follow that leader in an improvisatory manner.

j. The main tune/head (heard in extract A) is likely to return

TEST 11

Elbow: 'One Day Like This' from *The Seldom Seen Kid* 0:00–1:20, 3:15–4:44

a. 4/4 (accept 2/4)

b. One

c. They play a melody in octaves

d. Any two from:

- String part at the start foreshadows the vocal melody heard in the second part of the extract
- Lead singer and strings alternate melodies, like question-and-answer phrases
- Strings hold long notes while the lead singer sings
- Strings copy the lead singer in the second part of the extract
- Strings and voices play the same pattern together near the end of the extract ('Looking like a beautiful day').

e. Any two from:

- Lead singer joined by backing singers
- Voices in harmony (in 3rds)
- Melisma on the word 'day' (the rest of the extract is syllabic)
- Voices slide down (glissando) on the word 'day'.

f. **i.** [musical notation] **ii.** Ostinato (riff)

g. Possible answers include:

- Lead and backing vocals singing together, with quite a thin vocal texture at first but then gradually getting thicker with more layers of harmony
- Vocal echo introduced (after the word 'right')
- Backing vocals continue with the main tune while the lead singer introduces a different tune (heard earlier in the full song) in counterpoint…
- …And he starts very high, giving a more intense feel
- A heavier, more sustained bass line enters
- The harmonies change
- There is a guitar countermelody
- The drum part becomes busier, with fills at the end of phrases.

TEST 12

Extract A – 'Bubaran: Nudan Mas' from *Java Court Gamelan*   1:03–2:08
Extract B – Handel: 'Glory to God in the highest' from *Messiah*   0:54–1:53

a. i. Gamelan   **ii.** Oratorio

b. i. Pélog   **ii.** Major

    Characteristically, only five of the seven notes in the scale are used in *Bubaran: Nudan Mas*.

c. Indicative answers include:

	Extract A	Extract B
How are the performers most likely to have learned the music?	By ear, sitting alongside a more experienced player and copying – through the oral/aural traditions.	From written music notation (perhaps backed up by listening to recorded performances).
How do the performers stay in time together and know when to change tempo or dynamics?	The drummer usually leads the group and signals changes in dynamics/tempo. The large gong marks the end of each cycle. Players listen carefully to each other and respond to aural signals.	By following a conductor who beats time and indicates changes in dynamics/tempo through visual signals and cues.
What sort of venue or environment is this music most likely to be performed in?	Credit for answers that show understanding that this music is likely to be part of something wider than a purely musical performance, such as puppet shows, ceremonies, rituals, dance, drama, etc. (Although gamelan is also performed in western concert settings.) This piece, being a 'bubaran', is used as an ending piece while the audience is departing, or as an encore in a western-style concert.	At a formal concert in a concert hall, church or similar venue. Usually a purely musical event.

TEST 13

Extract A – Schumann: 'Ich grolle nicht' from *Dichterliebe*	0:00–0:59
Extract B – Handel: Concerto Grosso in D, Op. 6 No. 5 (Menuet)	1:15–2:54
Extract C – Mozart: Piano Quartet in E♭ (Allegretto)	0:00–1:20

a.

Features of the instrumentation	
Strings, harpsichord, oboe and bassoon are heard	B
Piano and string instruments are heard	C
A continuo is heard	B
Number of performers	
There are two performers	A
There are four performers	C
There are more than four performers	B
Other features	
This is an example of lieder	A
This is a concerto grosso	B
The music is performed in strict time but with a ritenuto at the end	B
Chromatic harmony is heard	A

b.

	Period of musical history	Reason for your choice
Extract A	Romantic	Chromatic harmony; use of rubato; deep range of piano used – not available in earlier eras; wide range of pitch and dynamics used; lyrical melody; sense of drama; sounds like Schubert/Schumann, etc.
Extract B	Baroque	Use of continuo; harpsichord; typical Baroque orchestra; sounds like Handel/Bach, etc.; clear use of repeated sections; dynamics changed on repeats; use of ornamentation; diatonic harmony.
Extract C	Classical	Use of piano (rather than earlier harpsichord); question and answer – balanced phrases; sounds like Mozart/Haydn, etc.; credit attempt to describe the Alberti bass and the use of appoggiaturas.

AREA OF STUDY 3: DANCE MUSIC

TEST 14

Lehmber Hussainpuri: *Phuchal* 0:00–1:24

a. Britain; Punjab

b. Possible answers include:

- Dhol or dhol-like sound
- Chaal rhythm
- Other traditional instrumental sounds associated with bhangra (which could be synthesised) such as: harmonium; garah (earthenware pot which makes the distinctive 'whoop whoop' sound); tumbi (one-stringed instrument producing the plucked melody heard at the end of the extract)

A tumbi can also be heard at the beginning of Panjabi MC's Mundian Tu Bach Ke, which was in the UK Top Ten when it was released.

- Shouts of 'hoi'
- Melodies based around (or in the style of) Punjabi folk melodies – narrow vocal range, revolving around a few notes
- Sung in Punjabi
- Mix of traditional Punjabi tunes and rhythms with western popular-music instruments, styles and music technology
- Fast tempo.

c. Possible answers include:

- Use of synthesisers (e.g. string sounds, electric piano)
- Use of drum machine
- Scratching
- Artificial record 'crackle' added at the start
- Many of the sounds are highly likely to be samples (e.g. the shouts of 'aha' and 'hoi')
- Use of FX on the vocals (really noticeable when the beat stops at 0:54)
- Use of mixing desk (or computer-based mixer) to balance all the different musical elements (and make the cut-down section at 0:54 sound quieter/more distant)
- Use of sequencer to loop musical segments and assemble them into an overall structure.

d. Possible answers include:

- Club-dance scene (especially, but not exclusively, in Asian communities)
- Asian weddings
- Bollywood films.

TEST 15

Flook: *Asturian Way*   0:00–0:31

a. **i.** AABB   **ii.** Binary

b. **i.** Flute; whistle   **ii.** They play the tune in octaves   **iii.** Guitar; bodhran

Some students may hear a bass, and there is a bass player in other tracks on this album. However, the bass sounds heard are almost certainly just the bottom notes of the guitar part.

c. Possible answers include:

- Feel of two beats in a bar (time signature of $\frac{2}{4}$, $\frac{4}{4}$ or $\frac{2}{2}$)
- Lots of fast quaver movement, with a few slightly longer notes (where you can often hear the performers snatching a breath)
- Fast, lively tempo with a bouncy feel
- Melody largely moving in small intervals, with a few leaps
- Fairly simple harmony
- Ornamentation on the melody
- *No credit for answers that simply repeat features from earlier questions.*

TEST 16

Extract A – Paul van Dyk: *For an Angel*   0:00–1:04

Extract B – Joe Arroyo: *Rebelión*   0:33–1:36

Extract C – Goldie: *Angel*   0:19–1:42

a.

	Extract A	Extract B	Extract C
Drum 'n' bass			✓
Trance	✓		
Salsa		✓	
The music is built entirely on a series of repeated loops, and panning is a major feature of the music	✓		(✓)
Son clave		✓	
Vocals have been overdubbed and treated with digital FX			✓
Vocals sung in Spanish – features a *prégon* and *choro*		✓	
The only vocals are a sampled, whispered 'For an angel'	✓		
Created entirely using music technology	✓		
Performed live with no use of music technology		✓	
Combines music technology with performers			✓

b. Extract B

c. **i.** Tiësto, Sasha, The Future Sound of London or any other trance musicians/DJs. It's actually Paul van Dyk.

ii. Joe Arroyo (which it is), Tito Puente, Eddie Palmieri, Fruko or any other salsa musicians

iii. Goldie (which it is), Roni Size, or any other drum 'n' bass artist

TEST 17

Gotan Project: *Santa Maria* 0:00–1:36

a.

b. Two

c. Possible answers include:

- Typical tango instruments: bandoneón (accordion); bass; piano
- Minor key
- Typical tango rhythms (especially clear in the rhythmic part that starts at 0:08)
- Steady dance tempo of around 120 beats per minute
- Jerky rhythms with lots of staccato notes
- Snare drum rolls to emphasise start of new phrases
- Characteristic run (on piano) up to the chords to signify the start of new phrases
- Heavily emphasised, punctuated chords.

d. Possible answers include:

- Use of samples (e.g. the vocal samples)
- Use of electronic sounds (e.g. the insect effect; the 'swish' sound that marks the start of phrases)
- Layering of percussion sounds as the track progresses – overlay
- Use of digital FX to transform sound, e.g.:
    - Echo/delay on the chords
    - Reverb/distortion on vocal samples (telephone effect)
    - Electronic treatment of acoustic sounds (e.g. the characteristic tango rhythm that enters at 0:08 and is then heard all the way through – probably originally created on a muted/deadened acoustic guitar).
- Mixing desk used to balance sounds
- Panning used to place them across the stereo spectrum
- Drum-machine loops.

e. Possible answers include:

- Solid four beats in a bar fits with tango dance movements
- Suitable dance tempo for tango, at around 120 beats per minute
- Clear phrase structure
- First beat of each bar very clear
- Jerky rhythms and staccato style match the movements of the dance
- Passion and intensity of the music reflect the style of the dance.

TEST 18

Extract A – Billy Ray Cyrus: *Achy Breaky Heart* — 0:00–1:11
Extract B – Tchaikovsky: 'Danses des cygnes' from *Swan Lake* — 0:00–0:52

	Extract A	Extract B
Type of dance	American line dance	Waltz
Time signature	$\frac{4}{4}$	$\frac{3}{4}$
Harmony	■ Chords change very slowly – typically one chord lasts for four bars before changing ■ Built around only two chords – tonic and dominant ■ Major chords/major key.	■ Chords change quite slowly (typically every one or two bars, apart from the longer one-chord introduction) – but faster than extract A ■ Much wider variety of chords used (including minor chords) than in extract A ■ Major key (like extract A) but… ■ Modulates to a minor key for last section.
Instruments used	■ Electric guitar (lead guitar and rhythm guitar) ■ Bass guitar ■ Drum kit ■ Tambourine ■ Vocals ■ Piano (playing chords very quietly in the background during the chorus).	■ Full orchestra, with… ■ Tunes played by strings and woodwind (flute, oboe, clarinet, bassoon) ■ Brass instruments not so prominent but accompany the tune.

Dance steps and movements used	■ Dancers stand in lines, facing the same way
	■ Men and women in any order – no physical contact
	■ All perform same steps at the same time
	■ Variety of steps such as 'boot scoot', 'stomp' 'heel dig' and 'grapevine'
	■ Credit for reference to features of the dance structure such as:
	  ■ Basic (one run through of the dance in its simplest form)
	  ■ Restart (where the basic sequence is interrupted and the dance routine started again from the beginning – used to fit the steps with the phrasing of the music)
	  ■ Walls (the direction the dancers face at the end of one sequence of steps).
		■ Danced by male/female partners facing each other, in close embrace
		■ Three-step dance sequence: forward (or backward) – side – together, repeated over and over so that couples rotate around the dance floor
		■ Also more ambitious steps such as spins and turns
		■ Smooth, graceful movements
		
		Some students may recognise that this is actually ballet music, and if so may make slightly different responses.

TEST 19

Bee Gees: *Night Fever*   0:00–1:25

a. Possible answers include any four from:

- $\frac{4}{4}$ time
- Characteristic drum pattern with: bass drum on every crotchet beat; snare on beats 2 and 4; quaver hi-hat rhythm
- Melody on string instruments
- High, sustained string sound
- Tempo near to 120 beats per minute (it's actually closer to 110 beats per minute)
- Use of guitar with FX (wah-wah)
- Accept verse-chorus structure (although it's a bit more complex than this)
- Use of electric piano/synth
- Lead singer/backing vocals.

b. Possible answers include any three from:

- FX (wah-wah) on guitar (using FX pedal)
- Reverb on voices
- Delay/echo (e.g. at end of extract)
- Use of electric piano/synth
- Tone/timbre/frequency shift on long-held notes near end of extract (probably achieved using a wah-wah pedal)
- Accept use of drum machine (it's not, but could be)
- *Any other relevant points, but beware of double crediting answers already given for question (a).*

c. Possible answers include:

- Dancers often do their own moves, on their own
- Dancers often wave arms or make arm gestures
- Dancers often remain on one spot
- Sometimes there are set routines that develop for particular songs (reference to John-Travolta type movements).

d. Bee Gees or other suitable performers

TEST 20

Extract A – Lúnasa: *Mi Na Nollag*   0:00–0:29

Extract B – Flook: *Asturian Way*   1:32–2:02

a.

Time signature	
$\frac{6}{8}$ time	A
$\frac{2}{2}$ time	B
Type of dance	
Reel	B
Jig	A
Instruments	
Violin/fiddle	A
Guitar	Both
Bodhran	B
Other features	
Major key	Both
Binary form	Both

You can also hear uilleann pipes (and flute) playing in extract A.

b. Credit for reference to:

- Repetition
- Putting together a collection of short tunes (in the same or similar dance styles) to make a longer sequence.

Extension suggestion

Listen to the whole tracks to hear how different tunes are strung together. Ask students how many different, complete tunes they hear on each track.

c. Ireland

TEST 21

Lehár: *Gold and Silver*   1:17–2:30

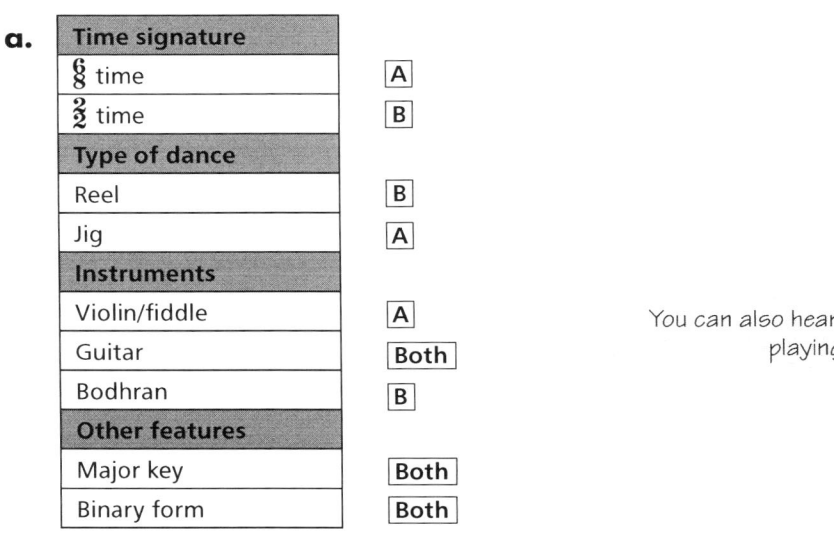

AREA OF STUDY 3: DANCE MUSIC

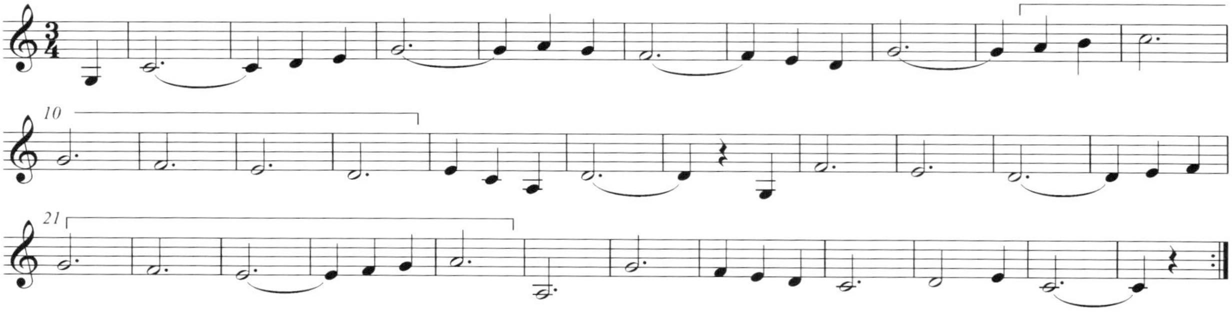

b. Interval of an octave

c. **i.** Imperfect   **ii.** Perfect

d. Plays arpeggios/broken chords/regular quaver patterns

e. Waltz

f. Any three from:

- Three beats in a bar
- Um-cha-cha pattern (bass note on beat 1, chords on beats 2 and 3)
- Credit for reference to very slight Viennese lilt – second beat slightly anticipated
- Flowing melody
- Slow harmonic rhythm – no more than one chord per bar.

g. Vienna

h. Strauss, or another suitable composer (it's actually Lehar)

TEST 22

Extract A – Klaus Badelt: *He's a Pirate*   0:00–1:30
Extract B – Tiësto: *He's a Pirate (Tiësto Remix)*   3:15–4:43

a.

b. Possible answers include:

- Fast tempo suits fast-paced action
- Simple tunes (revolving around a few notes) sound like sea songs
- Driving percussion gives a sense of excitement
- String instruments play the tunes in a staccato and rhythmic fashion – gives a forceful and driving feel to the music
- French horns on the tune (later on in the track) give a 'nautical' feel
- Percussion towards the end – the bass drum roll and the way the cymbals are used – replicates sound of the sea (crashing waves, etc.)
- *Any other suitable points that link musical features to features of a pirate movie.*

c. Possible answers include:

- Elements from the original (master) recording
- Transformed into a different musical style
- Chopped up and re-ordered
- Combined with new musical ideas
- Combined with a new and different beat.

d. Possible answers include:

- Computer sequencer used to isolate, combine and re-order elements of the original master recording with new ideas
- Overdubbing used to place new material over the original recording
- Multi-tracking used to build the whole piece
- Sampler used to extract elements of the original recording
- Use of synthesisers for new melodic ideas (that shadow some of the tunes from the original recording)
- Use of drum machine to provide the main beat of the remix
- Layering of drum-machine sounds
- Digital FX (reverb and echo/delay) used to give a different feel to the original track
- Massive reverb on the stab chords
- Reverb on synthesiser sounds
- Mixing desk used, for example: to balance the original recording so that it sounds distant in the mix; to fade the dance beat out and then back in; to balance the original track and the new material (e.g. at 4:01–4:15, where there is a drum fade in and transition from the original material to a new synthesised version of the original)
- Looping used for the repetitive dance beats and patterns
- Panning used: to separate sounds across left and right speakers; to give the effect of movement by bouncing sounds from one speaker to the other
- *Any other suitable points that link musical features heard with appropriate technology.*

TEST 23

Sonora Carruseles: *Micaela*   3:02–4:45

a. Salsa

b. Any two from: Spain; Cuba; Puerto Rico; Columbia (or other Latin American countries); New York; Africa

c. Swing rhythms

d. i. Riff   **ii.** Eight   **iii.** Doubled an octave higher; last note held on for longer with a crescendo

e. Credit not given for answers that simply repeat features mentioned as part of questions (c) and (d), unless they show a greater depth of understanding. Possible answers include:

Vocals	<ul><li>Call and response</li><li>Lead singer (*sonero/prégon*) and chorus (*choro*)</li><li>Chorus sing in close harmony – have repeated refrain</li><li>Lead singer improvises in the gaps between the chorus</li><li>Sung in Spanish.</li></ul>
Piano	<ul><li>Plays repeated (syncopated) pattern/ostinato virtually all the way through.</li></ul>
Bass	<ul><li>Plays repeated (syncopated) pattern/ostinato virtually all the way through</li><li>Pizzicato/plucked.</li></ul>
Brass	<ul><li>Trumpets...</li><li>Play characteristic repeated patterns at the start and end of the extract</li><li>Sometimes in unison, sometimes in close harmony</li><li>Solo trumpet in call-and-response pattern with the choro</li><li>Characteristic fall from high notes (glissando effect)</li><li>Very high playing at times.</li></ul>
Percussion	<ul><li>Typical salsa percussion instruments: timbales; congas (note how they improvise and get a bit more elaborate at times, e.g. towards the end); guiro/scraper; can also hear handclaps, cymbal, tambourine</li><li>Different instruments play different interlocking (syncopated) rhythms</li><li>Percussion breaks near the end of the extract.</li></ul>

TEST 24

Astor Piazzolla: *Libertango* 0:56–2:05

a. Any three from:

- Bandoneón (accordion)
- Strings/violins
- Bass
- Allow credit for reference to the *orquesta tipica*, even though this extract features a bigger ensemble than the classic tango band.

b. Any four from:

- Steady pulse, with four beats to the bar ($\frac{4}{4}$ or $\frac{2}{4}$)
- Syncopated rhythms
- Minor-key harmony
- 'Spiky' accompaniment, with staccato notes, reflecting the style of the dance movements

- Regular phrase lengths in the melody
- Credit for reference to characteristic tango rhythm heard in the accompaniment:

c.
- Partner dance – in close embrace
- Quick/sharp walking movements
- Upper body upright, with most of the movement coming from the dancers' legs
- Intertwining of dancers' legs.

d. i. Any one point from:

- Incorporation of elements from classical music and/or jazz
- More academic approach: could be concert music, not just for dancing
- A wider range of instruments compared to the traditional tango bands
- Credit also for references to later developments such as the electronic influence on electro tango.

ii. Astor Piazzolla (credit for other suitable composer of tango)

AREA OF STUDY 4: DESCRIPTIVE MUSIC

TEST 25

John Powell: 'Berlin Foot Chase' from *The Bourne Supremacy* 0:45–1:42, 2:41–3:58

a. **i.**

    ii. One or more octaves lower than written

b. **i.** Strings *(there is also a piano)* **ii.** Ostinato; trills

c. ♩ = 80

d. Exactly the same

e. Possible answers include reference to:

- More complex texture
- Drum part is much busier
- Deep, growling synthesised bass part at start
- Strings play similar patterns to those in extract A, but using double-speed repeated notes that give the effect of tremolo
- High trills on strings
- Use of crescendos, e.g. with cymbals and with strings just before the key change
- Change of key half way lifts tension
- Generally louder, partly because more is going on
- Strings playing much higher than in extract A (more use of extremes of range in general)
- Accents/stabs on strings, especially near the end
- Strings playing faster runs near the end (although overall tempo still the same)
- Repeated high notes with dissonances, and crescendo from strings at end.

f. Possible answers include:

- Drum patterns created using drum machine/sequencer – use of loops/looping
- Synthesised instruments playing melodic parts, e.g. phat bass part at start of extract B
- Electronic sounds that come in over the basic patterns, such as: hooting sounds; flapping sounds; metallic sounds
- Use of electronic FX to treat sounds, e.g. reverb/distortion on bass and electric guitar
- Use of sampler (e.g. to treat the drum track)
- Piano may be synthesised/sampled (but could be 'live').

g. Many possible answers here. Credit for answers that show understanding of:

- Timings and levels of dramatic tension set by on-screen action, so composer will have had to match their score carefully to this, probably in discussion with the film's director
- Music almost certainly put together initially using music technology/sequencer, and tempo/structure adjusted so that timings match the film's key points

- Live instruments then recorded on top of either this music-technology backing or a click track, with the players wearing headphones as well as watching a conductor (who may also be watching the film at the same time)
- Music technology (sequencer/mixing desk) then used to mix the live and synthesised/electronic sounds, add electronic FX as appropriate, and then balance the music against the film's dialogue and sound effects.

TEST 26

Randy Edelman: 'A Call to Adventure' from *The Mummy: Tomb of the Dragon Emperor*   0:20–1:14

a. See score above

b. Strings/violins; brass/French horns

c. See circled notes on score above

d. Many possible answers, including any three from:

- Driving $\frac{6}{8}$ rhythms and moderately fast tempo – sounds exciting as well as fun
- Major key and largely diatonic harmony give bright, optimistic feel
- Heroic sounding brass/French horns
- Use of rising arpeggios in the tune gives a fanfare-like feel
- The introduction has repeated rhythm patterns, trills and a crescendo – rising sense of excitement
- Repeated quaver pattern in accompaniment gives a strong sense of movement – almost feels like horse-riding rhythms, gives sense of fun
- Harp glissando near the end of the introduction gives sense of excitement
- Cymbal crashes and snare drum rhythms give a sense of excitement
- The tune is an octave higher when played the second time – even more uplifting.

TEST 27

Vaughan Williams: Symphony No. 7 (Prelude) 1:26–3:20

In this sort of question, students will gain marks for using correct musical terminology and for accurate spelling, punctuation and grammar. There are numerous possible points to be made, including reference to:

- Music at the start of the extract gives the sense of a heroic struggle by:
    - Starting quietly followed by a big crescendo to a climax
    - Starting low in pitch but then rising to the climax.
- The climax near the start is on a major chord, but is surrounded by elements from minor (modal) scales, giving a heroic but ominous feel
- Fairly slow tempo and the timpani rolls at the first climax give the sense of people struggling to put one foot in front of the other
- Dissonant harmonies give a sense of unease/danger
- Use of xylophone/piano/harp – brittle/icy sounds
- Long, quiet string and woodwind melody has high and low instruments playing in octaves (actually across six octaves): gives a feeling of loneliness/emptiness
- Use of ostinato/repeated ideas – gives the sense of a landscape that goes on forever without changing
- Wordless female voices give sense of loneliness/desolation – sound like the wind howling
- Tremolo strings give a sense of menace/sound like shivering
- Regular low drum stroke under the female voices gives a sense of doom/like a funeral drum.

TEST 28

Saint-Saëns: *Danse Macabre* 0:43–2:25

a.

b. Any two from:

- Played by full string section (instead of solo violin)
- Played in octaves
- Fuller accompaniment (e.g. woodwind instruments on the off-beats, sounding at a higher pitch compared with original pizzicato strings)
- Louder.

c. Xylophone

d. Counterpoint; fugue; a variation on a melody heard earlier

e. Possible answers include:

- Xylophone sounds like bones rattling

AREA OF STUDY 4: DESCRIPTIVE MUSIC

- Waltz style suits the idea of the dance of Death: um-cha-cha patterns used at times
- Solo violin playing harsh, eerie harmonies/oddly tuned at times
- Fugue entries at end like skeletons coming out of the ground one at a time
- Use of part of the chromatic scale (as in the main violin melody) gives an eerie effect
- Minor key prominent – gives a gloomy effect
- At times the music alternates between a minor and major feel, giving an unsettled effect
- *Any other appropriate comment linking a musical feature to an aspect of the story.*

TEST 29

Extract A – Marco Beltrami: 'Main Title' from *Hellboy*   0:00–1:08

Extract B – Marco Beltrami: 'Hellboy and Liz' from *Hellboy*   1:51–2:46

Extract C – Marco Beltrami: 'Stand by Your Man' from *Hellboy*   1:07–2:34

a. i.    **ii.** Anacrusis (accept upbeat)

b. i. Largo   **ii.** Diatonic   **iii.** Changes key just for the last chord

c.

	Extract A (main Hellboy theme)	Extract B (main love theme: Hellboy and Liz)
Use of tempo and rhythm	■ Effect of someone striding through the streets created by: ■ Bass line rhythms giving a sense of direction and purpose ■ Bass drum playing on beats 1 and 3.	■ Slow tempo and regular rhythms – makes it sound as though the characters are secure and happy with each other.
Use of melody and harmony	■ Sense of strangeness is portrayed by: ■ Chromatic harmony ■ Harmony alternating between a major and minor feel and... ■ The melody shifting from minor to major versions of the same chord ■ The melody being made up of semitone shifts and awkward leaps. ■ The shape of the melody generally keeps rising – gives the feel of a heroic struggle.	■ Melody moves largely by step, in scale patterns – gives a gentle effect ■ Generally diatonic harmony, giving a stable, settled feel ■ Rocking movement in the accompaniment and the fact that the melody gradually gets higher gives a forward, driving momentum that creates a sense of passion ■ Long-held notes that fall create a sense of tension (and resolution) that feels a little sad.
Use of instruments	■ Bell sound at start gives a sinister feel ■ Walking electric bass line gives a cool feel to the character ■ Brass (French horns) playing the melody sounds quietly heroic ■ Strings/trumpets play the melody later – even stronger heroic feel ■ 'Plodding' timpani/bass-drum part gives impression of a larger-than-life character.	■ Use of a traditional orchestra makes the music sound less 'offbeat' than in extract A: the characters are in love, just like ordinary people ■ Melody on strings gives a romantic feel ■ Held brass chords underneath give a sense of stability and security, although... ■ The heavy timpani/percussion on the first beat of the bar is a little threatening.

d. Possible answers include any two from:

- Faster tempo
- Melody in a different key – allows the horns to sound more strained and heroic than they did at the start of extract A
- Accompanied by different, driving rhythms – makes it sound more aggressive and forceful
- The melody develops into a more conventionally heroic style, with fewer odd leaps than in extract A
- Odd, sinister version heard at the end on tremolo strings.

TEST 30

Ron Goodwin: 'Where Eagles Dare (Film Theme)' from *Where Eagles Dare* 0:00–1:27, 1:28–3:09

a. i. Snare drum/side drum

ii. [rhythm notation]

b. i. Strings   **ii.** Fugue

c. i. pianissimo/*pp* (accept piano/*p*)   **ii.** fortissimo/*ff* (accept forte/*f*)

d. i. Starts in a minor key, modulates through several different keys and ends in a minor key

ii. Starts in a minor key, modulates through several different keys and ends in a major key

e. Many possible answers, including:

- The World War II setting is reflected in:
    - The military sounding rhythms (including rolls) on snare drum
    - The march-like feel to the music, in $\frac{2}{4}$ time.
- The complex story, where nobody is quite sure what is happening, is reflected in:
    - The fugue, with lots of different instruments coming in with separate entries and then interweaving
    - The many changes of key, giving a sense of uncertainty.
- There is a feeling of danger, created by:
    - The use of low dark sounds from brass instruments near the start (after the snare-drum passage) of extract A, and string instruments at the start of extract B
    - Minor-key feel for most of the music – especially at the start of each new section (although it does modulate a lot).
- The idea of people fighting to overcome impossible odds is reflected in:
    - Most of the tunes start low and keep rising in pitch
    - Both extracts start (very/fairly) quietly and then build to a climax.

f. Bear in mind that answers should not solely duplicate answers to other questions. Possible answers include:

Similarity:
- The military snare-drum rhythms are used in both extracts
- The exact snare-drum rhythm from the start of extract A comes back very loudly near the end of extract B (transferred to other instruments as well)
- Same tempo
- Both extracts start (very/fairly) quietly and build to a climax
- Some of the melodies/chord sequences are very similar/the same (e.g. the end of extract B references extract A clearly).

Difference:
- The snare-drum solo starts extract A and then dominates – in extract B it is silent at first and gradually works its way back into the texture
- Extract A has a mainly homophonic/chordal texture; extract B has a mainly contrapuntal/polyphonic texture
- The climax to extract A is on a minor chord and has a dark feel; extract B builds to a dramatic, sustained climax in the minor before reaching a triumphant major-key climax.

TEST 31

Extract A – John Williams: 'The Planet Krypton' from *Superman: The Movie*		0:18–1:22
Extract B – John Williams: 'Lex Luthor's Lair' from *Superman: The Movie*		0:00–1:30
Extract C – John Williams: 'Prelude and Main Title March' from *Superman: The Movie*		3:59–4:54

a.

	Extract A	Extract B	Extract C
Diatonic melody and harmony, stays in same key throughout	✓		
Mainly diatonic melody and harmony, changes key for different sections			✓
Chromatic melody and harmony, keeps making odd jumps to different keys		✓	
Tune played by brass, accompanied by this rhythm heard over and over again: ♩. ♫ ♫ ♫ 𝄾 ♫ ♫ ♫			✓
Main tune played largely by woodwind instruments and tuba		✓	
The flow of the music is interrupted several times by snarling sounds on brass instruments		✓	
A slow, gradual crescendo	✓		
Compound time signature			✓
Canon and imitation	✓		

b. Possible answers include:

Character/place	Which extract?	Features of the music that make it dramatically effective
Superman, faster than a speeding bullet, able to fly, a symbol of hope	C	<ul><li>Major key/diatonic harmony sounds full of hope</li><li>Compound rhythms and fast tempo sound exciting and joyous</li><li>Tunes based around tonic/dominant notes give a sense of strength (fanfare-like)</li><li>Repeated dotted rhythm really drives the music on, sounds exciting</li><li>Fanfare-like orchestration: melodies on brass instruments sound positive and confident.</li></ul>
The villain Lex Luthor and his rather incompetent assistants	B	<ul><li>Shifting keys, chromatic melody/harmony and fact that the tune and accompaniment sound like they don't fit, gives a sense of being untrustworthy/unreliable/a bit twisted</li><li>Slightly comic march patterns and tunes fit the incompetent assistants</li><li>Muted brass snarls give a sense of something really nasty</li><li>The music never really gets going – contrast to the driving, upbeat Superman theme.</li></ul>
The majestic main city on the planet Krypton	A	<ul><li>Slow stately tempo and gradual crescendo give a sense of grandeur</li><li>Slow crescendo/thickening texture give the sense that the city gradually comes into view</li><li>Loud climax feels as though you can see the whole city</li><li>Major key, diatonic harmony make it sound like an uplifting place</li><li>Brass fanfare-like tunes make it sound majestic.</li></ul>

TEST 32

Grieg: 'In the Hall of the Mountain King' from *Peer Gynt Suite No. 1*　　　　　　0:00–2:09

a.

b. Pizzicato

c. Possible answers include:

Tempo of the music	■ Starts at a moderate speed ■ Gradually accelerates during the course of the piece, reflecting the increasing panic ■ Ends up very fast.
Use of pitch	■ Melody played at a low pitch to begin with (at lower octaves than printed in the test) – sounds like someone sneaking around in the dark ■ Entirely low-pitched sounds at the start ■ Melody played at increasingly higher pitches as the music progresses, giving an increasing sense of excitement ■ At the climax the very high pitch of the melody gives the effect of panic ■ Towards the climax the full range of the orchestra is used, from low to high, as though the full company of trolls is chasing the hero.
Use of dynamics	■ Quiet at the start, as the hero tiptoes around ■ The music gradually gets louder, as though more and more trolls are waking up, increasing the excitement ■ Sudden accents (followed by silences) and crescendos towards the end, as though the Mountain King is almost catching the hero but just missing.
The way the instruments are used	Numerous possible answers. Credit for reference to: ■ The dark sound of low instruments at the start (bassoon and lower strings)… ■ With occasional muted brass notes giving a sinister effect ■ Pizzicato violins take over the tune, alternating with clarinets/oboes. Other instruments accent beats 2 and 4 (lower strings with a sinister 'burr'/ornament) ■ Strings play the tune arco and tremolo towards the climax – gives a stronger effect and a sense of panic ■ Much more use of brass and percussion add to the excitement as the music moves to the climax ■ Leading up to the climax the horns play long notes on beats 1 and 3, with woodwind/brass/cymbals on beats 2 and 4, driving the music forward ■ Woodwind/brass/strings/cymbals create sudden accented crashes in the last section – as though the hero is almost getting caught ■ Timpani-roll crescendo just before the final crash – sounds like the final dramatic climax ■ The music starts with a thin two-part texture, just melody and bass, and the texture gets busier and more complex as the music progresses, reflecting increasing panic.

d. Grieg or another similar 19th-century composer

TEST 33

John Barry: 'Capsule in Space' from *007: You Only Live Twice*   0:00–2:46

a. Ostinato

b. Possible answers include:

- Very slow, repeated timpani pattern heard at the start – sounds eerie and empty
- Quiet gong at the opening gives an eerie, airless feel
- Solo flute plays a slow melody with long notes (then taken over by string instruments) – sounds like floating
- Arpeggio/broken-chord patterns (on harp and vibraphone) outline unusual, chromatic harmonies/ unrelated chords, giving an unworldly feel
- The recording uses lots of reverb (or is recorded in a very large, resonant room), giving the feel of being in a vast, open space
- Tremolo strings at the end of the extract, gradually fading away as the astronaut disappears into the depths of space
- *Any other relevant comments linking musical features from the extract with space.*

c. Possible answers include:

- The slow tread of the timpani, and the fact that the music is based almost entirely on ostinati, gives a relentless feel to the music – something is approaching that you can't escape from
- Starts with one ostinato (timpani) and then gradually adds more on top (harp/flute, then brass) so that the music becomes more complex as it proceeds, adding to the tension
- The brass ostinato starts at a low pitch but goes up an octave after every two cycles, adding to the tension
- The music starts quietly and gradually gets louder as more instruments are added (e.g. brass chords are added underneath the brass tune)
- Although the basic tempo stays about the same, the melodic lines have shorter note values as the extract proceeds and so feel as if they are moving at a faster pace (the timpani ostinato is in semibreves, the flute tune is in semibreves and minims, the trumpet ostinato is in minims, crotchets and quavers, etc.)
- The actual climax is the tensest moment, achieved by:
    - Additional percussion coming in (cymbal crash and triangle)
    - The pacing of the music appears to increase as the music loops after only the first part of the brass ostinato – a two-bar rather than four-bar cycle (the actual tempo doesn't change)
    - This shortened brass ostinato starts low and goes up an octave on each repetition
    - There is a new, high and fast-moving string ostinato
    - The harp plays fast glissandos
    - Loud, sustained minor chord near the end, with brass, drum roll and tremolo strings – probably the loudest moment in the extract.
- *Any other relevant comment that shows how musical features from the extract increase tension.*

d. It's actually John Barry (a very distinctive sound) but accept any other suitable film composer such as Jerry Goldsmith, John Williams, etc.

TEST 34

Mussorgsky: 'The Gnome' from *Pictures at an Exhibition* 0:49–2:21

a. Minor key, chromatic harmony

b. Possible answers include:

The tempo of the music	■ Lots of sudden changes of tempo... ■ ...Alternating between a moderate slow speed (accept moderato or andante)... ■ ...And much faster (presto/vivace)... ■ ...Gives the effect of a creature lurking and then suddenly darting somewhere else.
The use of dynamics	■ In the first part of the extract: 　■ Starts moderately loud/moderately quiet with a series of short crescendos and decrescendos – gives a sense of brooding menace, like the gnome sitting somewhere in the shadows waiting to pounce 　■ Where the music suddenly changes to the faster sections: louder dynamic ending with sudden accents – makes you jump as the gnome moves. ■ In the middle of the extract, a more sustained loud section sounds like the menace is much closer – gradual diminuendo at the end of this section, as though the menace is retreating into the shadows again ■ Music goes quiet (towards the end of the extract) and then builds through a fairly long crescendo. This builds tension, as you are not sure where the menace is (You know it's somewhere ... You can hear it ... It's coming closer ... It's here!)
The way that the instruments are used *No credit just for naming instruments – students need to show how they are used to create the effect*	■ At the start legato, eerie sounds on brass and wind contrast with the higher pitched, more staccato strings – contrasting sinister and aggressive moods ■ Loud timpani/drum strokes and sometimes other percussion (xylophone) used to accentuate the end of the sudden fast sections – adds to the surprise effect of this sudden movement ■ Muted brass instruments give a sneering/snarling effect ■ String instruments play tremolo – gives a sense of fear ■ Trills on low woodwind instruments and drum rolls give a sinister, menacing effect towards the end ■ On top of these trills a combination of woodwind, muted brass, xylophone and pizzicato strings create a sinister dance feel – as though the gnome is toying with people ■ Just before the final fast section, the music builds up to a loud dissonant chord – you can hear the muted brass clearly, though strings are there as well: sounds as though this is where you realise how nasty the gnome actually is.

c. i. Very resonant recording/reverberation (accept echo)

　ii. *Either* by being recorded in a big, resonant venue *or* by adding digital reverb FX

This is an orchestration of Mussorgsky's Pictures at an Exhibition by Leopold Stokowski, and is quite different to the more common Ravel orchestration. If you have a recording of the Ravel orchestration, it might be worth asking students to compare the two, to spot the differences, and to discuss which is more effective.

CROSS AREA OF STUDY QUESTIONS

TEST 35

Extract A – Sonora Carruseles: *Micaela*   0:00–0:45

Extract B – Berlioz: 'Marche au supplice' from *Symphonie fantastique*   5:42–7:02

Extract C – Ravi Shankar: 'Raga Mishra Gara: Gat in Fast Teen Taal' from *Spirit of India*   3:49–5:03

a. Salsa

b.

Shouts and claps	Piano and guiro	Bass, congas and timbales	Brass	Backing vocals	Lead singer

c. Possible answers include:

- Usually a paired dance (male/female partners)
- Loose embrace or hold hands
- Four-beat patterns: dancers step forwards and backwards together, or out to the side and back
- Additional turns, spins and holds
- Upper body remains fairly static, but hips move a lot
- Movements reflect the syncopated rhythms of the music.

d. Possible answers include:

Section of the story	How the music portrays the story
Prisoner carried in a marching procession up to the guillotine	<ul><li>Minor key creates sombre effect</li><li>March tempo and dotted rhythms give the feel of the (almost military) procession</li><li>Sudden, loud brass chords and cymbal crashes give a sense of finality – no escape</li><li>Dotted rhythms on strings (and brass) sound desperate</li><li>Music shifts rapidly from one repeated chord on brass and wind to a totally unrelated repeated chord on strings (at 6:07) – sounds unsettled</li><li>Just before the solo clarinet (in the next section) loud chords build up to an imperfect cadence – gives a sense of expectation.</li></ul>
The crowd goes silent, he thinks for one last time of the one he loves ... The guillotine comes down and beheads him	<ul><li>Solo clarinet plays the tune* – sounds lonely, thinking of his loved one</li><li>Loud chord represents the guillotine</li><li>Pizzicato notes may sound like the head rolling into the basket.</li></ul> *Some students may have studied this piece and know that this tune represents the artist's loved one – the idée fixe of the symphony – although there is no extra credit for having studied this particular piece previously.
The crowd rejoices	<ul><li>Major key – the crowd is happy</li><li>One major chord repeated over and over again on brass and wind – the crowd is happy</li><li>Loud drum roll goes right through, with cymbal crashes at the end – celebration/ the crowd clapping and cheering.</li></ul>

e. India

f. Sitar; tabla; tanpura

g. Drone

h. ☐B The musicians will have learned this music from written music notation

☐C The musicians are improvising with raga and tala patterns

☐A The musicians will have learned the repeated patterns by ear, with some improvisation from soloists in call-and-response sections

TEST 36

Extract A – Ladysmith Black Mambazo: *Nikosi Sikelela*	1:47–3:04
Extract B – Saint-Saëns: *Danse Macabre*	5:05–6:14
Extract C – Tiësto: *He's a Pirate (Tiësto Remix)*	4:01–5:23

a. A cappella; call and response; male voices

b. **i.** Slows down (especially towards the word 'Africa', then picks up a bit before slowing down again at the end)

ii. By practising, getting to know the music really well from memory, and listening very carefully to each other.

This group is the famous Ladysmith Black Mambazo, whose leader gives various cues and signals as well.

c. Africa

d. Many possible answers, including:

- Fast dance tempo ($\frac{3}{4}$) fits the idea of a dance – like a demented waltz
- Accept reference to the long, rising scale at the start being like skeletons coming out of their graves (although that actually happens earlier in the complete piece)
- Minor key gives a sinister feeling to dance patterns that are normally more cheerful
- Obsessive use of rhythm patterns (♩ ♫ ♫ and ♫ ♫ ♩) give a feeling of being surrounded by scary things
- Brass and percussion (cymbals) burst in loudly several times – like skeletons suddenly jumping out at you
- The strings play fast, dashing-scale/broken-chord/sliding patterns, like skeletons dashing all over the place
- The music accelerates to represent the dance getting wilder
- At the climax, one chord is repeated over and over again, as though in a frenzy
- Near the end, the music suddenly stops, there is a change of key and tempo, and an oboe plays a tune like a cock crowing – dawn has come

- At the end a long held chord (with tremolo strings and a drum pattern underneath) gradually dies away, like skeletons sinking back into the ground.

e. **i.** Accelerates towards the climax, then suddenly changes to a much slower tempo (when the cock crows)

   ii. The performers watch a conductor, who controls the tempo with hand/arm gestures

f. Several possible answers, including:

- Use of samples (e.g. part of original *Pirates of the Caribbean* soundtrack; sword sounds)
- Remix of original music
- Music starts without a heavy drum beat, builds up to a climax quickly increasing in dynamic, then the steady, thumping bass-drum beat kicks in

This is really characteristic of trance – a build up where everybody in the club has their hands in the air, and then go wild when the drums kick in!

- Steady, thumping bass-drum beat
- Steady tempo, $\frac{4}{4}$ time
- Use of electronic sounds
- Lots of repetition/looping of ideas.

g.
- There is no change of tempo
- There are no live performers – the track is built up using music technology.

FULL TRACK LISTING

AREA OF STUDY 2: SHARED MUSIC

Test 1
Beethoven: Piano Concerto in G, Op. 58 No. 4, Andante con moto (0:00–0:44, 1:25–2:53)
Alfred Brendel, Simon Rattle, Wiener Philharmoniker; *Beethoven: Piano Concertos No. 1 & No. 4*

Test 2
Handel: Concerto Grosso in D, Op. 6 No. 5, Menuet (0:00–1:15)
Academy of St. Martin in the Fields, Iona Brown; *Handel: Concerti Grossi Op. 6 Nos. 5–8*

Test 3
Miles Davis: 'Freddie Freeloader' from *Kind of Blue* (0:21–1:30)
Miles Davis; *Kind of Blue*

Test 4
A. Schumann: 'Das ist ein Flöten und Geigen' from *Dichterliebe* (0:00–1:07)
B. Schumann: 'Ich grolle nicht' from *Dichterliebe* (0:43–1:40)
C. Schumann: 'Aus alten Märchen winkt es' from *Dichterliebe* (0:00–0:55)
Matthias Goerne, Vladimir Ashkenazy; *Schumann: Dichterliebe; Liederkreis, Op. 24*

Test 5
'Bubaran: Nudan Mas' from *Java Court Gamelan* (0:00–2:08)
Various; *Java Court Gamelan* (Explorer series)

Test 6
Mozart: Piano Quartet in E♭, Allegretto (7:36–8:47)
Emanuel Ax, Isaac Stern, Jaime Laredo, Yo-Yo Ma; *Mozart: Piano Quartets*

Test 7
Alexandra Burke: *Hallelujah* (0:00–1:02, 1:58–3:37)
Alexandra Burke; *Hallelujah*

Test 8
Ravi Shankar: 'Raga Mishra Gara: Gat in Fast Teen Taal' from *Spirit of India* (0:00–1:25)
Ravi Shankar; *Spirit of India*

Test 9
Handel: 'Glory to God in the highest' from *Messiah* (0:00–1:06)
London Symphony Chorus, London Symphony Orchestra, Colin Davis; *Handel: Messiah*

Test 10
Arnie Somogyi's Ambulance: 'Captain Courageous' from *Accident and Insurgency* (0:00–1:25, 4:40–6:20)
Arnie Somogyi's Ambulance; *Accident and Insurgency*

Test 11
Elbow: 'One Day Like This' from *The Seldom Seen Kid* (0:00–1:20, 3:15–4:44)
Elbow; *The Seldom Seen Kid*

Test 12
A. 'Bubaran: Nudan Mas' from *Java Court Gamelan* (1:03–2:08)
Various; *Java Court Gamelan* (Explorer series)
B. Handel: 'Glory to God in the highest' from *Messiah* (0:54–1:53)
London Symphony Chorus, London Symphony Orchestra, Colin Davis; *Handel: Messiah*

Test 13
A. Schumann: 'Ich grolle nicht' from *Dicheterliebe* (0:00–0:59)
    Matthias Goerne, Vladimir Ashkenazy; *Schumann: Dichterliebe; Liederkreis, Op. 24*
B. Handel: Concerto Grosso in D, Op. 6 No. 5, Menuet (1:15–2:54)
    Academy of St. Martin in the Fields, Iona Brown; *Handel: Concerti Grossi Op. 6 Nos. 5–8*
C. Mozart: Piano Quartet in E♭, Allegretto (0:00–1:20)
    Emanuel Ax, Isaac Stern, Jaime Laredo, Yo-Yo Ma; *Mozart: Piano Quartets*

AREA OF STUDY 3: DANCE MUSIC

Test 14
Lehmber Hussainpuri: *Phuchal* (0:00–1:24)
Lehmber Hussainpuri; *The Biggest Bhangra Hits, Vol. 1*

Test 15
Flook: *Asturian Way* (0:00–0:31)
Flook; *Haven*

Test 16
A. Paul van Dyk: *For an Angel* (0:00–1:04)
    Paul van Dyk; *For an Angel 2009 (All Mixes)*
B. Joe Arroyo: *Rebelión* (0:33–1:36)
    Joe Arroyo; *Greatest Salsa Classics of Colombia, Vol. 1*
C. Goldie: *Angel* (0:19–1:42)
    Goldie; *Timeless*

Test 17
Gotan Project: *Santa Maria* (0:00–1:36)
Gotan Project; *La Revancha del Tango*

Test 18
A. Billy Ray Cyrus: *Achy Breaky Heart* (0:00–1:11)
    Billy Ray Cyrus; *20th Century Masters – The Millennium Collection: Best of Billy Ray Cyrus*
B. Tchaikovsky: 'Danses des cygnes' from *Swan Lake* (0:00–0:52)
    Orchestra of the Mariinsky Theatre, Valery Gergiev; *Tchaikovsky: Swan Lake*

Test 19
Bee Gees: *Night Fever* (0:00–1:25)
Bee Gees; *The Ultimate Bee Gees*

Test 20
A. Lúnasa: *Mi Na Nollag* (0:00–0:29)
    Lúnasa; *Lúnasa*
B. Flook: *Asturian Way* (1:32–2:02)
    Flook; *Haven*

Test 21
Lehár: *Gold and Silver* (1:17–2:30)
Slovak Radio Symphony Orchestra; *Viennese Favourites, Vol. 1*

Test 22
A. Klaus Badelt: *He's a Pirate* (0:00–1:30)
Klaus Badelt; *Pirates of the Caribbean: The Curse of the Black Pearl*
B. Tiësto: *He's a Pirate (Tiësto Remix)* (3:15–4:43)
Tiësto; *Elements of Life*

Test 23
Sonora Carruseles: *Micaela* (3:02–4:45)
Sonora Carruseles; *Heavy Salsa*

Test 24
Astor Piazzolla: *Libertango* (0:56–2:05)
Astor Piazzolla; *Tutto Piazzolla: Il Re del Tango*

AREA OF STUDY 4: DESCRIPTIVE MUSIC

Test 25
John Powell: 'Berlin Foot Chase' from *The Bourne Supremacy* (0:45–1:42, 2:41–3:58)
John Powell; *The Bourne Supremacy*

Test 26
Randy Edelman: 'A Call to Adventure' from *The Mummy: Tomb of the Dragon Emperor* (0:20–1:14)
Randy Edelman; *The Mummy: Tomb of the Dragon Emperor*

Test 27
Vaughan Williams: Symphony No. 7, Prelude (1:26–3:20)
Waynflete Singers, Christopher Dowie, Lynda Russell, Kees Bakels, Bournemouth Symphony Orchestra; *Vaughan Williams: The Complete Symphonies*

Test 28
Saint-Saëns: *Danse Macabre* (0:43–2:25)
Charles Dutoit, Philharmonia Orchestra; *Saint-Saëns: Danse Macabre*

Test 29
A. Marco Beltrami: 'Main Title' from *Hellboy* (0:00–1:08)
B. Marco Beltrami: 'Hellboy and Liz' from *Hellboy* (1:51–2:46)
C. Marco Beltrami: 'Stand by Your Man' from *Hellboy* (1:07–2:34)
Marco Beltrami; *Hellboy*

Test 30
Ron Goodwin: 'Where Eagles Dare (Film Theme)' from *Where Eagles Dare* (0:00–1:27, 1:28–3:09)
Ron Goodwin & His Orchestra; *That Magnificent Man and his Music Machine: Two Sides of Ron Goodwin*

Test 31
A. John Williams: 'The Planet Krypton' from *Superman: The Movie* (0:18–1:22)
B. John Williams: 'Lex Luthor's Lair' from *Superman: The Movie* (0:00–1:30)
C. John Williams: 'Prelude and Main Title March' from *Superman: The Movie* (3:59–4:54)
The London Symphony Orchestra; *Superman: The Movie*

Test 32
Grieg: 'In the Hall of the Mountain King' from *Peer Gynt Suite No. 1* (0:00–2:09)
Berliner Philharmoniker, Herbert von Karajan; *Grieg: Peer Gynt Suites, Holberg Suite – Sibelius: Finlandia, Tapiola, Valse Triste*

Test 33
John Barry: 'Capsule in Space' from *007: You Only Live Twice* (0:00–2:46)
John Barry; *007: You Only Live Twice*

Test 34
Mussorgsky: 'The Gnome' from *Pictures at an Exhibition* (0:49–2:21)
Bournemouth Symphony Orchestra, José Serebrier; *Mussorgsky, Stokowski: Transcriptions*

Test 35
A. Sonora Carruseles: *Micaela* (0:00–0:45)
Sonora Carruseles; *Heavy Salsa*
B. Berlioz: 'Marche au supplice' from *Symphonie fantastique* (5:42–7:02)
London Symphony Orchestra, Colin Davis; *Berlioz: Symphonie fantastique*
C. Ravi Shankar: 'Raga Mishra Gara: Gat in Fast Teen Tal' from *Spirit of India* (3:49–5:03)
Ravi Shankar; *Spirit of India*

Test 36
A. Ladysmith Black Mambazo: *Nikosi Sikelela* (1:47–3:04)
Ladysmith Black Mambazo; *Live at Montreux: 1987, 1989, 2000*
B. Saint-Saëns: *Danse Macabre* (5:05–6:14)
Charles Dutoit, Philharmonia Orchestra; *Saint-Saëns: Danse Macabre*
C. Tiësto: *He's a Pirate (Tiësto Remix)* (4:01–5:23)
Tiësto; *Elements of Life*

COPYRIGHT

Rhinegold Education is grateful to the following for permission to use printed excerpts from their publications:

One Day Like This. Garvey/Potter/Potter/Turner/Jupp. © 2008 Salvation Music Ltd (NS). All Rights administered by Warner/Chappell Music Publishing Ltd. All Rights Reserved.

One Day Like This. Words and Music by Guy Garvey, Craig Potter, Mark Potter, Peter Turner and Richard Jupp. © 2008 Salvation Music Ltd, Warner/Chappell Music Publishing Ltd. Reproduced by permission of Faber Music Ltd. All Rights Reserved.

He's a Pirate. Words and Music by Klaus Badelt, Hans Zimmer and Geoffrey Zanelli. © 2004 Walt Disney Music (USA) Co, Warner/Chappell Artemis Music Ltd. Reproduced by permission of Faber Music Ltd. All Rights Reserved.

Gold and Silver Waltz – Franz Lehar. © Copyright 1904 by Glocken Verlag Ltd. Reproduced by permission of Boosey & Hawkes Music Publishers Ltd.

Where Eagles Dare. Music by Ron Goodwin. © 1968 Ole Grand Films, EMI Music Publishing Ltd. Reproduced by permission of International Music Publications Ltd (a trading name of Faber Music Ltd). All Rights Reserved.

'Berlin Foot Chase' (from *The Bourne Supremacy*). Music by John Powell. © Copyright 2004 Universal/MCA Music Ltd. All Rights Reserved. International Copyright Secured.

'A Call to Adventure' (Theme from *The Mummy 3*). Music by Randy Edelman. © Copyright 2008 Universal/MCA Music Ltd. All Rights Reserved. International Copyright Secured.

For An Angel. Words & Music by Paul Dyk Van & Johnny Klimek. © Universal Music Publishing MGB Ltd. All Rights Reserved. International Copyright Secured.

Hallelujah. Words & Music by Leonard Cohen. © Copyright 1984 Sony/ATV Music Publishing (UK) Ltd. All Rights Reserved. International Copyright Secured. Used by permission of Music Sales Ltd.

Santa Maria (del Buen Ayre), Hellboy (Main Title). Every endeavour has been made to trace the owners of the rights to these songs, without success.